trotman

REAL LIFE ISSUES:
CONFIDENCE
& SELF-ESTEEM

REAL LIFE ISSUES

Real Life Issues are self-help guides offering information and advice on a range of key issues that matter to teenagers. Each book defines the issue, probes the reader's experience of it and offers ways of understanding and coping with it. Written in a lively and accessible style, Real Life Issues aim to demystify the areas that teenagers find hard to talk about, providing honest facts, practical advice, inspirational quotes, positive reassurance, and guidance towards specialist help.

Other titles in the series include:

REAL LIFE ISSUES:
CONFIDENCE
& SELF-ESTEEM

Nicki Household

Real Life Issues: Confidence and Self-esteem
This first edition published in 2004 by Trotman and Company Ltd
2 The Green, Richmond, Surrey TW9 1PL

© Trotman and Company Limited 2004

Editorial and Publishing Team
Author Nicki Household
Editorial Mina Patria, Editorial Director; Rachel Lockhart, Commissioning Editor;
Anya Wilson, Managing Editor; Bianca Knights, Assistant Editor
Production Ken Ruskin, Head of Pre-press and Production
Sales and Marketing Deborah Jones, Head of Sales and Marketing
Advertising Tom Lee, Commercial Director
Managing Director Toby Trotman

Designed by XAB

British Library Cataloguing in Publication Data
A catalogue record for this book is available from the British Library

ISBN 0 85660 993 5

Typeset by Tradespools Publishing Solutions
Printed and bound in Great Britain by
Cromwell Press, Trowbridge, Wiltshire

CONTENTS:

'... one of the secrets of becoming a can-do person is to like and accept yourself just as you are.'

REAL LIFE ISSUES:
Confidence and Self-esteem

ABOUT THE AUTHOR

Nicki Household is a freelance writer specialising in health, relationships, consumer affairs and education. Following a degree in English Literature at Bristol University, Nicki trained and worked as a teacher of English as a Foreign Language before beginning her journalistic career with the *Reader's Digest*.

In two decades of journalism she has been a regular contributor to *The Times* and *Sunday Times, Radio Times, Woman's Weekly,* the *Daily Mail* and *The Times Educational Supplement*. Her previous books include career and consumer guides and she is the author of several BBC booklets about health and well-being. Nicki lives in west London and has a grown-up son and daughter and three cats.

REAL LIFE ISSUES:
Confidence and self-esteem

ACKNOWLEDGEMENTS

Thanks to Young Minds, North Wales Adolescent Service, the Royal College of Psychiatrists and the Mental Health Foundation for their advice and guidance in the preparation of this book.

And a very special thank you to all the young people who generously shared their own experiences, especially Kate, Alex, Matt and Dave (not their real names, but they know who they are!).

INTRODUCTION
What are confidence and self-esteem?

It's tougher than ever being a teen. People seem to expect so much more from you than they did when you were 'just a kid', but you don't yet have the freedom and independence that go with being an adult. It's a time of getting to know yourself, of recognising what you're good at and thinking about what kind of work you want to do, what kind of people you like and how you want to live your life. It's also the time when you begin to realise that your future is in your own hands.

Some lucky people sail through this tricky 'between' stage without too many problems. They may not be high-fliers or especially cool, clever, sexy or talented, but they do have a secret, and that secret is that they feel OK about themselves. So they're able to join in with group activities, make friends, express their thoughts and opinions, start new interests and generally enjoy life. They are 'can-do' people.

A can-do person hopes for the best in any situation, but can also deal with the odd mistake, rejection or failure. They see minor setbacks and disappointments as a normal part of life and most definitely *not* as something that 'always' happens to them because they're so 'rubbish'. The reason they're able to do this is because basically, deep down, they like and approve of themselves. They believe they deserve good things, and this helps them bounce back quicker.

The way you think about yourself is absolutely crucial to your confidence and self-esteem – and often has nothing to do with the *reality* of who or what you are. Some people who seem to have everything going for them can have a really low opinion of themselves, while others who, on the face of it, haven't got much to boast about may think they're fantastic! Believing you're wonderful is fine (though it may get on other people's nerves!), but thinking the opposite – that you're not as good/interesting/clever/lovable/attractive as other people – can stop you doing all sorts of things you'd really love to do.

Confidence and self-esteem are very closely linked. **Self-esteem** means 'valuing yourself'. When you have self-esteem, you are:

- happy to be who you are
- aware of your own strengths and achievements
- not too upset by criticism
- able to ask for what you want
- able to say how you feel
- able to laugh at yourself
- not easily put down – and unlikely to put others down.

Self-esteem is not the same as being cocky or seeing yourself as the greatest person in the world. And it certainly doesn't mean you can't be modest. It simply means thinking as highly of yourself as you do of the people around you.

Confidence usually comes from self-esteem. It means feeling sure of yourself and not being too nervous, scared or self-conscious in everyday situations. A confident person is:

■ comfortable with other people
■ able to communicate
■ able to enjoy themselves
■ happy to take on challenges
■ self-reliant
■ able to admit mistakes
■ able to accept help
■ not worried about looking foolish.

Few people feel as confident in their teens as they did when they were a child, so it's not at all unusual to find you're more shy or awkward than you used to be. This often happens because you're still getting used to the physical and emotional changes of puberty and are not yet sure who this 'new person' in the mirror actually is. The good news is that it's often just a temporary thing that vanishes as you get more used to the idea of yourself as a young adult. But occasionally, for a variety of reasons (see Chapter 3), it doesn't vanish, and that's when it's important to become aware of the kind of things you are saying to yourself – probably without knowing it.

This book is all about happily accepting that you are YOU – a unique and valuable person who deserves to be loved and appreciated, especially by you yourself! Because one of the secrets of becoming a can-do person is to like and accept yourself *just as you are.* Not fatter, not thinner, not taller, not shorter and with the same hair, ears, legs, nose, personality, talents and abilities that you have.

Of course, no one feels 100-per-cent terrific about themselves all the time – we all have moments of self-doubt. But basic confidence and self-esteem are important because they help you relate well to other people, so you can enjoy the fun times *and* find the support you need when the going gets tough.

The aim of the book is to:

- help you identify whether your confidence and self-esteem could do with a boost
- explain how other people, and even you yourself, may have contributed to any bad feelings you may have about yourself
- help you identify and appreciate your strengths
- suggest confidence-boosting techniques that *really work*
- tell you where you can go for further help.

'I've been through no money, been through violence, through this, that and the other. It's not something I choose to promote, it's something I've been through.

'I don't feel like I've got anything to be ashamed of. I'm myself and that's it. If I say something someone doesn't like, that's just tough. I'm not trying to offend anybody and if I do, that's their problem.

'In my life generally, I've been lucky to have intelligent, loving people around me who will take five minutes to teach me things about myself without preaching at me, just showing me naturally.'

Ms Dynamite (aka Niomi McLean-Daley), singer

CHAPTER ONE:

SELF-ESTEEM QUIZ
What do you really think of yourself?

Self-esteem is all about valuing yourself. It's easier to do this if you are aware of your strengths and achievements and happy to be the person that you are. Self-esteem helps you deal much more easily with hassles and put-downs, and it enables you to express how you feel and ask for what you want.

SELF-ESTEEM QUIZ

What do you really think of yourself? Your answers to this quiz will reveal all. Put a tick next to the answers that are *closest* to how you feel.

1 *Do you worry a lot about what other people think of you?*

a Yes, it makes me very anxious

b Never

c Not a lot

2 *Do you feel uncomfortable or self-conscious around other people?*

a Yes, I find it very hard to be myself

b What, *moi?*

c Only when I think they're judging me

3 *Does fear of failure ever stop you doing things you'd really like to do?*

a Yes, all the time

b I'll have a go anyway

c Sometimes

4 *Do you make friends easily?*

a No, I find it hard because people aren't friendly towards me

b Yeah, I've got dozens of them!

c I can make friends with people I like

5 *How do you feel if someone criticises you?*

a I hate it – it makes me feel miserable and worthless

b I'll listen, but I don't care

c I don't like it, but sometimes it's helpful

6 *Do you need other people's approval in order to feel good?*

a I wish I had other people's approval, but I never get it

b Not really – I'm quite a happy carefree person

c I need the people closest to me to think well of me

7 *When someone puts you down or tries to bully you, what do you do?*

a I pretend not to care but get very angry and upset inside

b I do the same back, but with knobs on

c I stand my ground and tell them to get lost

8 *Do you enjoy socialising and meeting new people?*

a It scares me so I try to avoid it

b Love it

c Yes, usually

9 *Do you think other people are better off or luckier than you?*

a They definitely are

b Not really

c Sometimes

10 *Do you think you are less confident than other people?*

a Yes, I know I am

b No

c Only in some situations

11 *Are you able to put your own views across in an argument?*

a No, because I don't like disagreeing

b Yes, and I always do

c I can if I feel strongly enough

12 *Can you talk about your feelings to people?*

a I don't think anyone is interested

b I'm always expressing my feelings

c I can to a few people

13 *Do you feel you deserve love and respect?*

a I'd like to deserve it, but I'm not sure I do

b I'm sure I do

c I think I do

14 *How do you feel about speaking or performing in public?*

a Out of the question, I'd make a fool of myself

b Love it!

c I get nervous, but I'll do it if I have to – and then I enjoy it

15 *How do you feel about your physical appearance?*

a I just wish I looked different – it's my hair/nose/weight/legs/skin/
height …

b I'm happy with my body, warts and all, and I take good care of it

c I'm OK about it, though there are things I'd change if I could

16 *Do you feel bad about doing or saying what you want?*

a Yes, because I don't feel I have the right to

b Not for a moment

c No, not if it doesn't hurt anyone

17 *Can you admit to your own mistakes?*

a Not very easily

b It doesn't bother me

c Sometimes

18 *Do you enjoy being yourself?*

a No, I often wish I was someone else

b Being me is just fantastic!

c Yes, most of the time

19 *Can you motivate yourself to do things?*

a No, I always think there's no point

b Try and stop me!

c Yes, with a bit of effort

20 *Are you proud of your achievements to date?*

a What achievements?

b I'm the best, no kidding!

c Yes, I've done quite a lot of good things

HOW TO SCORE THE QUIZ

Go through the questions and count up how many *as, bs* and *cs* you chose. There are 20 questions, and you've probably got a fair mix of all three. If, however, you've got many more of one than another, it tells you quite a lot about the way you see yourself.

A high '*a*' score – say, 12 or more – indicates that you are quite hard on yourself. You'll feel a lot better when you've worked on your confidence and self-esteem. Keep reading this book!

Twelve or more *b*s show that you have a very positive self-image (*too* positive, some might say!) and feel more than ready to face the challenges of life. If all 20 of your answers were *b*, give this book to someone else who really needs it.

Twelve or more *c*s show that you feel really good about yourself, but are not a super-confident extrovert. You don't need to work on your self-esteem unless you still feel there were too many *a*s.

'You have to be happy with who you are. I wasn't always popular in school or with boys, but I always liked who I was anyway.' **Britney Spears, singer**

CHAPTER TWO

DO YOU THINK TOO LITTLE OF YOURSELF?
Some signs of low self-esteem

When you feel good about yourself, the world seems a friendly place. You hold your head up high, you *expect* people to be nice to you – and you don't even care too much if sometimes they aren't! You're able to bounce back because your deep-down sense of yourself is positive. You know (as all of us should) that you are a unique and valuable individual with your own talents and strengths.

But when your basic attitude towards yourself is not so great, you're likely to think more negatively about things. You may even expect events to go badly for you and feel defeated by small setbacks. Some of the reasons why young people can get into this negative way of thinking are explained in Chapter 3, but this section concentrates on the signs and signals – things you may be doing and thinking which suggest that your opinion of yourself is (for whatever reason) on the low side.

First of all, it's important to say that we all get mad at ourselves from time to time, especially when we do something silly or embarrassing. It only becomes an issue if you *always* expect to mess up, or if you've persuaded yourself that you're not as good – or as lovable – as other people. Negative thoughts and attitudes like these are like 'the enemy within', and it's important to recognise and disarm them because they can spoil your enjoyment of life.

LISTEN OUT FOR NEGATIVE MESSAGES

Once you become aware of them, you will be able to spot negative messages not only in the things you think and feel, but also in the way you behave. Here are two examples of the kind of situations that may bring them out:

1 They're casting a school/college musical and you'd really love to be in it. But you don't tell anyone or put your name on the list because a familiar little voice inside is saying something like:

- I haven't got the courage
- I'll let myself down
- The others are all better than me
- People will laugh at me.

2 There's someone you'd really like to go out with, or at least get to know better. But you're not even going to risk being friendly towards them in case they:

- tell you to get lost
- think you're desperate
- snigger about it with their friends.

In situations like these, people who feel reasonably OK about themselves tend to have a 'can-do' attitude. They may not ooze confidence, but they have enough belief in themselves to give it a go. They'll audition for the show, accepting that they may or may not be given a role. If they succeed – great. If not, well at least they tried and probably learnt something from the experience that will give them a better chance next time.

It's the same in the relationship situation. Knowing you are a valuable person in your own right gives you the courage to ask someone out. It also enables you to cope more easily with the situation if they tell you they'd rather stay in and wash their hair! You see their reply for what it is – a minor setback – and not as conclusive evidence that you are completely unfanciable and are never going to have a boyfriend or girlfriend!

> **For a closer look at relationships, see**
> ***Real Life Issues: Sex and Relationships.***

Thinking you are doomed to failure and being afraid to try anything new are just two of the many ways some people with low self-esteem score 'own goals' against themselves. The chart below shows some of the typical thoughts and feelings of someone with low self-esteem and what is perhaps the corresponding reality.

THOUGHTS AND FEELINGS:	FACT:
Thinking everyone else is happier and more confident than you are	People usually behave more happily than they feel, so you can't tell much about their feelings
Not wanting to put any effort into things, because you 'know' you won't succeed	Of course you could succeed. But you won't know until you try
Labelling yourself 'dumb' every time you make some tiny mistake	Constant self-criticism only reinforces your negative view of yourself
Not giving yourself credit for the things you've achieved	You've done all sorts of good things. Try listing them
Being too timid to stand up for yourself when people put you down	Putting people down is in itself a sign of low self-esteem

THOUGHTS AND FEELINGS:	FACT:
Not liking your body because it's not perfect	No one's body is perfect. But yours deserves to be accepted and looked after
Wanting to avoid people because you feel safer on your own	Connecting with other people is an important part of learning to like yourself
Being too anxious to please	Of course you want to be liked, but your own personality and needs should not be suppressed
Refusing to accept compliments	A compliment means that someone wants to make you feel good – so let them!
Agreeing to things you don't really want to do	People will respect you for saying 'no' when you mean 'no'

When people *behave* in a negative way, this too can be a sign that they undervalue themselves. But because they come over as angry or bullying, the lack of self-esteem is less obvious. The way it works, according to psychologists, is that instead of taking your feelings of 'inferiority' out on yourself (though you may do that as well) you take them out on other people. In other words, you are just as unkind to others as you are to yourself. Because of this, people with low self-esteem will sometimes:

- lose their temper at the drop of a hat
- be quick to start a fight
- pick on other peoples' weaknesses
- blame other people for their own mistakes
- have nothing good to say about anyone or anything
- argue about everything
- enjoy hearing about other people's troubles.

Even dangerous behaviour like stealing, drug abuse and joy-riding can indicate low self-esteem, especially in cases where what it's really saying is: 'I'm not worth anything, so I don't care what happens to me or what anyone else thinks of me.' Unfortunately, however, low self-esteem is not seen as a valid excuse in a magistrate's court!

When people seriously undervalue themselves, their thoughts often form a vicious circle that keeps feeding on itself. Here's an example of a very negative pattern of thinking:

There's no point in me trying to achieve things, join in things or make new friends because I'll only fail or be laughed at or bullied.

I don't like myself... I'm hopeless, I look awful and I'm no good at anything – I don't deserve any attention.

I wish more nice things would happen in my life, but it's not surprising they don't because I'm so unattractive/clumsy/stupid/boring, etc.

I'm such a loser – no wonder I don't like myself...

In real life, not many people are quite as down on themselves as that! But when you lack self-esteem, there's a real risk of getting into a repetitive pattern of thinking that is not only wrong, but also prevents you enjoying life and growing as a person. More worryingly, it is also linked to teenage pregnancy, eating disorders, suicidal thoughts and long periods of unemployment. So it's very important to get out of a negative way of thinking. The best way to achieve this is to stop being so hard on yourself – and you'll find plenty of advice on this in Chapters 7 and 8.

FACT BOX

Low self-esteem used to be considered one of the main causes of drug and alcohol abuse, violent crime, racial prejudice and dangerous driving. But according to some new research the opposite is true. This kind of behaviour is actually more likely to be shown by people who have very high self-esteem. They say and do whatever they like because they think they are totally marvellous and other people 'don't matter'. So next time you meet a bully, tell them they're suffering from 'high self-esteem disorder'!

CHAPTER Three:

WHAT CAUSES A LOSS OF SELF-ESTEEM?
Nature or nurture?

Unfair though it seems, part of the difference between one person's self-esteem and another's is genetic – in other words, some people are just born pleased with themselves! But it's the things that happen *after* you are born that have the biggest influence.

The key words are **approval** and **acceptance**. By approving of someone you show that you believe they are good and worthwhile. By accepting them you show that you are happy for them to be a part of your life. So, naturally, if those two crucial things are missing while you are growing up, it's all too easy to start thinking – quite *wrongly* – that you're not worth much.

Usually, parents, teachers and carers try to do their best for young people and wouldn't deliberately want to hold back on approval and acceptance. But in some cases their own lives may be very difficult, and in others they may just not be aware that their behaviour is too critical or unaccepting.

Self-esteem can also be knocked by life events such as illness and parents arguing with each other or breaking up. Situations like that can make you feel helpless – as if you have no power over your own life.

Our self-esteem tends to go up and down in response to things that happen to us. For example, if you pass an exam or fall in love you feel great about yourself, but if you fail an exam or get dumped by someone you may think a bit less of yourself. But this feeling of low self-esteem probably won't last very long if you basically like and approve of yourself. It may take a little time to understand the situation and to accept it or find a way round it, but eventually you find you are back to your usual self.

It's this ability to bounce back that proves that your self-esteem is basically OK. But if bouncing back seems impossible (and this often happens if bad events pile up on each other), then it's important to take steps to build back your self-esteem. Fortunately, most of us manage to get through life feeling fairly positive about ourselves.

In the next few pages we'll look at some examples of the kinds of life events that can knock your self-esteem. At the end of this book, there's a list of useful organisations that you can contact if you need to talk about any of these issues further.

BECOMING ILL

Feeling weak or ill can affect your self-esteem, especially if you can't take part in activities with friends or have to spend time in hospital. Having an accident or getting ill can also make you feel as if your body has let you down and that you have no power over the situation you are in. And hospitals and institutions have a way of making you feel as if you are just a patient with a number, and not a lively individual with your own thoughts and feelings. At times like this, it becomes doubly important to feel able to express your personality and needs.

ALEX'S STORY

'I think the hardest thing is when people call you names and mutter behind your back. I've missed a lot of school because of an illness called ME which makes you feel really tired all the time. I've had people call me "diseased", and some boys were taking bets on whether I'd "bother" to turn up for lessons or not. I've found this really hard to cope with, and it makes me not say anything in class because I don't want to draw attention to myself. I don't want to be noticed or have people saying anything about me. My self-esteem is all right at home, but it's not good at school.

'Once, one of my friends explained to a teacher that I couldn't come to school that day because I was really tired and the teacher said: "Well, I feel pretty tired, too. Don't I deserve a day off as well?" I wanted to catch up with work at home and asked my teachers to email me work, but only one of them did. I couldn't really chase the others so I just left it.

'I've often felt really useless, as if I was slowing other people down. But luckily I have an amazing group of friends who look out for me and invite me everywhere, even though I often can't go. That's been the most important thing for me – having some people around who just accept me.' **Alex, 15**

CONSTANT CRITICISM

There is nothing wrong with occasional criticism, especially if the person is trying to help you. But if someone keeps picking on you and finding fault with everything you do, it can affect the way you think about yourself – even if you know deep down that their comments are unfair and not true. The person who's doing this may well have a self-esteem problem him/herself.

VIOLENCE

Real-life violence is very damaging to self-esteem. This may involve punishments where you are hurt and have no chance to fight back or it may be seeing people you love behaving violently towards each other. Sudden unexpected violence is extremely upsetting, but so is the 'lesser' kind that goes on for a long time, like constant pushing and bullying. Your self-esteem can also be affected by seeing someone you love insulted or treated with a lack of respect, or by feeling that your family aren't respected. It's important to talk to somebody you trust who is outside the violent situation.

SEXUAL ABUSE

Any kind of unwanted sexual activity or talk is very damaging physically and emotionally and is, of course, another form of violence. It is important for you that the situation should stop, so always report sexual abuse to someone you trust.

LOSING SOMEONE OR SOMETHING

Losing a person – or even a pet – who has been an important part of your world can have a devastating effect on your confidence and self-esteem. Obviously the worst thing is the death of someone you love, and you will need lots of time to mourn and to talk about this. But any kind of loss of something that's important to you – your home, perhaps, or a much-loved object, can affect the way you feel about yourself.

PARENTS' PROBLEMS

Your self-esteem can be knocked for six when it's actually your father, mother or other relative who has the more serious problem – for example, a relationship break-up, debt, losing a job, or something that makes them unreliable like drug or alcohol abuse.

> **For a closer look at drug or alcohol abuse, see**
> ***Real Life Issues: Addictions.***

A LOT OF BAD THINGS HAPPENING AT ONCE

Sometimes it can seem as if life has got it in for us. Shocks such as family break-up, redundancy, illness, bereavement, a serious accident or a relationship ending are hard enough to deal with when they come singly, but when two or more of them come together, it can make you feel as if someone has decided you just don't deserve to feel OK. You may even start thinking it about yourself.

But the fact is you *do* deserve to feel OK, and are simply going through a very tough time. Don't try to be big and brave and pretend you don't care. Get all the support you can from friends and family or talk to a counsellor.

FEELING NEGLECTED OR MISUNDERSTOOD

Even the most well-meaning parents may sometimes do things that can affect your self-esteem. For example, they may:

- leave you on your own for long periods or seem too busy to spend time with you
- give you the impression that they prefer your brother or sister to you
- insist on you learning or doing something that doesn't interest you, or prevent you taking up something that does
- ignore or not notice the way you feel about something

- discuss things that concern you in front of you (like schools or holidays) but not ask your opinion
- not tell you about important things that are happening like the fact that the whole family is moving to live 200 miles away
- blame or criticise you for things you haven't done.

It's not always easy to stand up for yourself and explain to parents or other adults how they are making you feel. But learning to be assertive (see Chapter 5) can help.

TIP BOX

It's a fact of life that teenagers complain about parents. They've always done it and they always will! And, to be fair, a lot of parents do seem to pay more attention to what their teens are doing wrong than to what they are doing right. But, believe it or not, parents themselves often feel misunderstood. There they are, doing their best, and all their teen does is criticise them. So why not try noticing what your parents are doing right *for a change. Start by making a list of all the useful things they do for you – like feeding you, paying for things, caring for you when you're ill, perhaps even lying for you when you haven't done your homework! And add to the list every time they do something right. You never know, they might start noticing a few things you're doing right as well!*

FAILING EXAMS OR GETTING LOW MARKS

Low marks for schoolwork can be upsetting, but if your self-esteem is good you don't mind so much because you are aware of all the other things you are good at, both inside and outside school. Exams and qualifications are useful, but not necessary for self-esteem, confidence or happiness.

MATT'S STORY

'I always felt OK until Mum and Dad split up. When it happened, I didn't want to tell people at school because most of the kids I hung out with had their mum and dad at home and I didn't want to be different. Mum and Dad kept on rowing even after my dad went away; they couldn't speak to each other without shouting and slagging each other off. It was awful, and it made me feel really bad about myself, like I wasn't as good as other people.

'In the end, the teachers and all knew, and I felt like I came from a bad family who were no good because that's what some people think. My schoolwork got really bad, and there were two lads in my class who used to say things about me and I wanted to tell them to get lost but I couldn't.

'Then I got talking to other kids with parents who'd split up or never been together, and they seemed OK, so it made me feel better. I still had my other friends so that was OK, and anyway Mum got much better and we talked about how I felt and everything. What helped me most was getting into the football team – that made me feel great.' **Matt, 13**

'I wasn't very good at school. I was just good at drama and music and stuff. I got two GCSEs out of ten. Teachers used to go on about how GCSEs are the most important thing in your life and you're going to struggle. But I was like: "I know what I want to do."' **Anthony from Blue**

CHAPTER FOUR

FEELING 'DIFFERENT'
And how to stop feeling bad about it

Everyone wants to fit in and feel accepted. This can be especially true for young people, who often feel pressure to look the same, talk the same – even *think* the same – as their friends or classmates. Later in life, some people go to great lengths to makes themselves seem as different and strange as possible, just because they want to stand out from the crowd! But if you're going through a stage of feeling shy or self-conscious, that's the last thing you want. You just long to blend in and be like everyone else.

THINGS THAT MAKE US FEEL 'DIFFERENT'

Some people feel insecure because of one particular thing that they think sets them apart from others. This may be:

- gender
- appearance
- family circumstances
- race, culture, ethnicity, religion

■ sexual orientation (being gay)

■ disability.

We'll look at each of these below.

Gender

It's very common to feel self-conscious when you're with a friend or group of friends of the opposite sex. As a young child, you take kids of the opposite sex for granted and hardly notice them, but this changes as you become more aware of sexual differences, differing interests and of the possibility that the other person may be judging you or even weighing up whether they fancy you or not. The 'easiness' you

TIP BOX

Feeling 'different' can make you imagine that other people don't want to know you when in fact they do – so don't always wait for other people to make the first move! It's easy to think other people are unfriendly or stand-offish when they are simply shy or embarrassed or don't know how to start a conversation with you. Breaking into a group of people who are already friends may be hard, but it's much easier to reach out and make contact with another person who may also be feeling lonely or a bit left out. So instead of giving in to feelings of exclusion, make a point of noticing who else needs a friend, and pluck up the courage to talk to them.

used to feel with them has gone, and it can be really annoying if you find yourself blushing or not behaving naturally.

Usually, as you get older, most of this awkwardness disappears – although no one feels totally relaxed on a first date or when chatting to someone they secretly fancy. Unless they are one of those few super-confident people who never doubt themselves for a second!

If you do go on feeling uncomfortable with the opposite sex in everyday situations, this could be connected with your overall self-esteem, because if you have a falsely low opinion of yourself (or your appearance) it's easy to imagine that other people agree with you.

Appearance

You may feel you are too tall or short, too fat or thin, or that your nose, legs, hair or toenails are unsatisfactory. People's bodies come in all sorts of shapes and sizes, and no one is perfectly happy with what they have. However, research has shown that most young people who think they are not attractive are quite wrong about their own appearance, while others who are not actually as nice-looking (but more confident), often consider themselves irresistible! It's all to do with how you feel about yourself inside. There is more about how to change your self-image (the way you feel about your appearance) in Chapter 10.

Family circumstances

Now, more than ever before, families come in all shapes and sizes. But it's still easy to feel that your family is 'different', even though someone else in the same situation may be perfectly cool about it. Parents may live together or not, and they may be married or single, or living with a partner of the same or the opposite sex. You may be an only child, part of a step-family, or you may be living with relatives or with adoptive or foster parents. None of these situations is unusual, but it can still make you feel self-conscious if your 'peer group' (the other kids you mix with) have a different set-up.

You may also feel different if your family can't afford to buy things that other families seem to have. This might be because times are hard, or because someone you live with is ill or unemployed or has been made redundant. Unfortunately our society attaches far too much importance to things like cars, designer clothes and the latest technology. It's odd because these items don't make anyone happy!

Race, culture, religion

You may feel self-conscious because there are very few kids in your class or where you live of the same race, culture, religion or ethnic group as you. Differences in looks, clothes, food, language and beliefs may cause other kids to treat you differently or even, possibly, to bully you. There is no excuse for this, but the reason may be that they have grown up surrounded by people who think like them and look like them, so they are very ignorant about people who are different and may even be a little scared of them.

Sexual orientation

A lot of kids who know they are gay feel forced to keep it a secret from friends and family because they don't want to be laughed at or called names. Even when you know people who accept the fact that you are gay, you may still feel self-conscious or 'different'.

> **For a closer look at this issue, see**
> ***Real Life Issues: Sex and Relationships.***

Levels of ability

Being different from the majority in any way can make you feel set apart. Perhaps you use a wheelchair to get around or are learning to deal with a stammer. Perhaps you need regular injections, or extra help in class because of some special difficulty. You may also feel different because you have been singled out to move up a class or to be helped to develop a special talent. Absolutely any 'difference' can make you sensitive to other people's comments and reactions.

WHAT CAN YOU DO ABOUT ALL THIS?

First of all, try to stop feeling bad about feeling bad. It's completely normal to want to fit in and be part of things, so don't beat yourself up about it. Also, remember that if people seem unfriendly, they are not reacting to you *personally*, but to their own stereotyped image of you, which is probably based on some half-baked idea that came from their great-aunt or -uncle.

When you find yourself feeling self-conscious, remind yourself that:

- each one of us is unique and valuable
- no one can see what you are feeling
- it's the differences that make human beings interesting (wouldn't it be boring if we were all the same?)
- other people, even those you feel 'different' from, are struggling with their own feelings of self-consciousness. No one ever knows what is going on inside someone else's head.

Some people try to cover up their discomfort by going all quiet and silent or by being over-the-top noisy and opinionated. Neither of these is a good idea – not saying anything can make you seem stand-offish or unfriendly, and saying too much can make you seem mouthy and aggressive.

In general, people feel comfortable around you if you feel comfortable around them. And the best way to achieve this is to start feeling comfortable about yourself. Chapters 7 to 11 are full of techniques that will help you. Don't expect instant results, but if you make it your aim to *keep building* your confidence and self-esteem, you will quickly get to a point where you feel a whole lot better about yourself and ready to make new friends and try new things.

However, feeling 'different' is always stressful, so make sure you regularly spend time in situations where you are automatically accepted or where people like you are in the majority. The 'outside world' is not always friendly, but hopefully there are places we can all go where we feel totally relaxed and comfortable.

YOU ARE YOU ... NOT SOMEONE ELSE!

We all present a better face to the world than the one that's hiding inside, which is why other people often seem happier and more successful than we are! Comparing yourself with other people is not good for your self-esteem – especially if the people you compare yourself to are TV presenters or pop stars who probably spend hours a week disguising their natural appearance!

Being a performer or a show-off is not the same as having self-esteem – as shown by the number of stars and celebrities who have drug, alcohol and relationship problems. The same is true the other way round. If someone is quiet and thoughtful and not keen to appear on *Big Brother* or try karaoke or pole-dancing, it doesn't mean they have no confidence or self-esteem. Lots of strong, secure people just don't enjoy these things and may even find them naff or silly. They know what they like and have no problem saying 'no' to things that don't appeal.

Admiring people is one thing. Comparing yourself to them and hating the fact that you're not like them is another. We are all different, and the person you really need to start admiring is … YOU!

KATE'S STORY

'I didn't feel good about myself as a teenager because I was bad at writing and spelling because I'm dyslexic. My work always came back covered in red marks even though I'd put a lot of effort into it. Some teachers used to say they didn't believe it had taken as long as I said it had, and they made me feel stupid. It was upsetting because I understood the lessons but just couldn't write things.

'Another side of it was that that I had a bad sense of rhythm and movement, like I was hopeless at skipping games because I couldn't make my body jump at the right time. I knew that if I got a chance to practise, I'd be OK, but when everyone's playing a game, there's no time for that. You want to show the world you can do it, and I knew that if only I could practise it ten times, I'd be as good as someone who'd only done it twice. It does make you lack confidence when you can't do things that other people find simple.

'But as I got older I realised that not being able to spell wasn't saying anything about me. I also discovered computers with spell-checks! Everyone is good at something, and you have to value it yourself. Also, it's important to have people around you who value it. My mum and dad always told me I was intelligent, and I was lucky to have some good friends who didn't mind photocopying their GCSE notes for me. In the end I got an English degree at university, and now I'm much more confident because I've learnt that self-esteem isn't about what other people think – it's something you have inside.' **Kate, 23**

CHAPTER FIVE:

MOTIVATION
Your inner fuel

When you decide to try something new, the hardest bit is getting started. There's something about venturing into unfamiliar territory or facing up to a challenge that makes many of us want to just turn on the telly or go back to sleep. It's like the feeling you get when you know you ought to tidy your room or start an essay. Just when you're about to start, you suddenly think of something else you've just got to do at once, like phone a friend, listen to some music or make a sandwich.

Self-motivation – or finding the energy to do things – is crucial to everything you want to do in your life. If you're lucky, you may have positive and supportive friends and family who give you ideas and help you get started. But in the end it's down to you because you can't always rely on others to encourage you. There may be things that no one else knows you want to do – such as strengthening your self-esteem. Also, there are times in life when we all have to face difficulties and challenges on our own, and that's when you need self-motivation to get you through.

The best kind of motivation comes from really *wanting* to do something, although we are also motivated by really *having* to do something. For example, no one really wants to get up early on a freezing cold winter morning and set off for school or work. You do it because there'll probably be trouble if you don't, and staying out of trouble is a kind of motivation. But the other, much more interesting, kind involves things we don't have to do, but which we've chosen to do because they will bring long-term benefits or satisfaction.

Watching telly, eating crisps, hanging out with friends or going to the pub don't count because things like that don't require motivation. Things that *do* count include:

- taking up a new sport
- trying a new hobby or activity
- joining a club
- helping at home
- learning to play an instrument
- reading a book
- cooking a meal
- changing the way we think about something.

These are all things that may seem like a bit of a sweat before you start, but which you really enjoy once you're into them and feel pleased about afterwards – unless you chose the wrong thing, like flower-arranging when you really wanted to take up football!

The last item in the list – changing the way we think about something – is a *project* in the same way that starting a new hobby or learning to play the guitar is a project. You have to be motivated to do it, which means having the inner will and enthusiasm to get started – and to keep going (whatever the difficulties).

If you feel you lack self-motivation, try listing one or two things you've done that you feel proud about. Forget any negatives and just concentrate on positive successes. Your list can include anything at all from, say, helping a friend get over a broken relationship to scoring a goal in a football game or learning a new skill. Can you remember how you felt about it at the time? You probably felt a strong sense of energy and determination. That feeling is still inside you somewhere, and getting in touch with it will help you find the motivation to start building your confidence and self-esteem.

ELIMINATE THE NEGATIVE

Motivation is all about feeling positive and optimistic, so it may help to identify any negative influences in your life. Make a separate list of any people you know who put you down or make you feel bad or who you feel are abusive towards you in any way. Hopefully, this list is empty. But if there is anybody doing this, they have problems of their own which may be affecting you. Their negative behaviour can drain away your positive energy and hold you back from feeling motivated.

Abusive people lower your self-esteem, and it's very important to get them right out of your life. People who put you down in other distressing ways such as bullying or constant criticism should also, if possible, be stopped. If this seems impossible, talk about the situation with someone you can trust. **Assertiveness techniques** may also help you stand up for yourself without being aggressive.

What is assertiveness?

Assertiveness is an attitude which says: 'I respect and value myself and I am happy to communicate with you as long as *you* respect and value me. I am also prepared to respect and value you, but I choose to set my own boundaries to protect myself.'

As well as being a way of thinking about yourself, it's also an effective way of relating to other people. Assertive people are firm, positive and optimistic, rather than scared, ashamed or apologetic. They ask rather than boss, and they don't lose their cool in an argument.

Assertiveness is closely connected to self-esteem. It means you can:

- say what you feel (without getting angry)
- tell other people what you want/don't want from them
- say 'no' to things you don't agree with
- resist 'peer pressure' to do things you don't want to do
- stand up for and take good care of yourself
- not 'give in' just to satisfy somebody else
- set your own boundaries and defend them
- give and receive compliments and criticism
- feel you have a right to enjoy life
- be a friend to others.

Being able to say 'no' is a very important part of self-esteem. Some people get a kick out of persuading others to do what they want. It could be anything from bunking off school to alcohol or drug abuse, unsafe sex, crime or vandalism. Remember the decision is always yours. 'No' can be a very positive word!

How is assertiveness different from aggression?

Aggression is all about forcing other people to do what you want by making them afraid to stand up to you, walk away or say 'no'. It is the opposite of being **passive**. A passive person finds it very difficult to stand up for what they want or believe. They tend to think 'anything for a quiet life' and let other people have their own way. Passive people can easily become victims.

Assertiveness is nothing like either of these. An assertive person doesn't want to control anyone else, but also doesn't want to be controlled. They defend their own space and are in charge of their own life. When necessary, they can also defend and stand up for other people.

GEMMA AND TRACY'S STORY

Gemma and Tracy shared a room, but had different attitudes to clutter. Gemma was really organised and always tidied things away at the end of the day. Tracy left everything from cold cups of coffee to yesterday's underwear lying exactly where she dumped it. Gemma resented this and from time to time had a rant about how disgusting and selfish Tracy was. Tracy would then accuse Gemma of being 'anal' and carry on chucking things on the floor. Often Gemma ended up tidying Tracy's clutter herself. Then, one day, she decided she'd had enough and put all Tracy's stuff in black bags by the bins. Tracy went ballistic, and that was the end of a beautiful friendship.

Neither of them had managed to be assertive. Tracy acted aggressively by taking up Gemma's space and being scornful about her neatness. Gemma alternated between aggression (when she ranted about how selfish Tracy was) and passivity (when she did Tracy's tidying for her). In the end, both behaved aggressively – Gemma, by dumping Tracy's things in the yard, and Tracy, by losing her rag and ending the friendship.

Both passive and aggressive people behave as if only one person counts. A passive person is saying, 'You matter and I don't,' but an aggressive person is saying, 'I matter and you don't.' *An assertive attitude says: 'I matter and so do you.'*

So what should Gemma and Tracy have done?

■ Tracy should have respected the fact that room was half Gemma's and kept her things tidy.

■ Instead of shouting and criticising, Gemma should have picked a moment when she and Tracy were both calm, and quietly explained that it really upset her to be surrounded by Tracy's mess and asked her to try to be tidier.

■ Between them, they might have succeeded in coming to an agreement without any insults.

■ The black bag incident would never have occurred, and Gemma and Tracy would still be friends.

But it does take practice to be calm and assertive when someone is annoying or upsetting you. A lot of people either bottle up their anger (passive) or erupt in fury (aggressive). Or else they totally ignore other people's rights (as Tracy did), which is another kind of aggression. The middle way is the assertive attitude that says: 'I matter and so do you.' Self-esteem will help you find that middle way.

The differences between assertive, aggressive and passive behaviour – in terms of body language – are summed up in the boxes below:

Assertive body language	**Aggressive body language**	**Passive body language**
■ Firm voice	■ Raised voice	■ Droopy shoulders
■ Good posture – body relaxed, head up	■ Threatening gestures	■ Weak trembly voice
■ Calm facial expression	■ Tense body	■ Avoiding eye contact
■ Direct, friendly eye contact	■ Angry facial expression	■ Sad or scared expression
	■ Staring people down	

'The secret of total gorgeousness is to believe in yourself, have self-confidence and try to be secure in your decisions and thoughts.'
Kirsten Dunst, actress

TIP BOX

If you find it hard to get motivated, have a chat to a positive friend or relative – someone energetic who always seems to get things done. Ask them how they motivate themselves. Then next time you decide to go for something, pretend you are that other person. Just try to behave as they would. This may seem strange and unreal to begin with, but after a while your own natural motivation will kick in and you won't feel the need to imitate anyone. But if ever you feel your motivation slipping again, go straight back into that 'other person' mode!

CHAPTER SIX:

SELF-MOTIVATION QUIZ
Do you need a bit more 'go'?

Self-motivation is central to everything you want to do in your life. It's even crucial to improving your self-esteem because if you really want to change the way you think about yourself, you first need the inner desire and determination to do it.

SELF-MOTIVATION QUIZ

The fact that you are reading this book proves you are already self-motivated. But this quiz will reveal whether you could do with just that bit more 'go'

1 *You've promised yourself you'll get up early on Sunday morning to do something. When the alarm goes off, do you stick to your plan?*
a Yes
b No

2 *Once you've started a project do you usually finish it?*
a Yes
b No

3 *Do you stick at things even when the going gets tough?*
a Yes
b No

4 *If something interests you, do you try to find out more about it?*
a Yes
b No

5 *Have you ever tried to teach yourself a new skill?*
a Yes
b No

6 *When you decide to do something, can you ignore the possibility that you might not succeed?*
a Yes
b No

7 *Do you know what you are best at?*
a Yes
b No

8 *Are you developing and improving the thing(s) you are best at?*
a Yes
b No

9 *Are you happy to make the first move towards a friendship or relationship?*
a Yes
b No

10 *Do you find it easy to ask for help or advice?*
a Yes
b No

11 *Do you set yourself goals that you think you can achieve?*
a Yes
b No

12 *Do you find it quite easy to ask people for things?*
a Yes
b No

13 *Do you know what job or career you want?*
a Yes
b No

14 *If 'yes', are you doing anything to make it a real possibility?*
a Yes
b No

How have you scored? Ten or more 'yes' answers show you have lots of self-motivation. An equal number of 'yes' and 'no' answers is about average. Ten or more 'no' answers show you may need to work on your get up and go!

CHAPTER SEVEN:

GET POSITIVE!
Building up your self-esteem

To succeed in building and hanging on to your self-esteem, you need to feed your brain lots of positive messages. Sometimes, when you're feeling low or unconfident, it's easy to do exactly the opposite and find yourself thinking something like:

Poor me, nothing ever goes right for me. My parents have split up/ my mum drinks/ my dad has gone away/ I haven't got any friends/ I'm rubbish at everything/ no one thinks I matter/ my life is no fun/ I'm destined to be miserable.

OK, that's a pretty heavy example of the 'poor me' syndrome. But negative thoughts about yourself can easily become a habit and rule your life.

Of course, lots of problems in life are very real, and you can't pretend they don't exist. But there is also a positive side to them because the way you overcome problems and the things you learn from them can help you grow and change. Often it's not the problems themselves that make your life miserable, but the way you let negative thoughts about them creep in and affect the way you feel about yourself.

These negative thoughts come from:

■ being too critical and judgmental about yourself
■ not giving yourself credit for all the good things you've *done* and all
  the good things you *are*
■ Taking other people's negative comments to heart.

If this sounds at all like you, the time has come to GET POSITIVE!

GIVE YOURSELF CREDIT

Your new way of thinking is going to start with a list of all your
achievements since the day you were born. This should be a long list
of all the good things you have ever done. At first, this may not be
easy because you've got so used to ignoring your strengths and
dwelling on your weaknesses.

First of all, include every early-life milestone like:

■ learning to smile (friendliness)
■ learning to crawl (curiosity)
■ learning to walk and run (energy)
■ learning to talk (communication)
■ learning to laugh (happiness)
■ learning to read and write (intelligence)
■ learning to draw or sing or dance (self-expression)
■ learning to tell jokes (sense of humour).

You may be able to think of many more – such as starting school
(coping with change), making a friend (liking/being liked), doing an
assembly (courage), winning a prize or a race (excelling) and so on.

Now move on to things you've achieved more recently. These might include:

- helping someone
- making something
- joining a club/group/team
- having fun/enjoying yourself
- completing a project
- getting a qualification
- passing an exam
- finding the courage to say or do something
- cheering someone up
- saving money to buy or do something you want
- getting yourself through a difficult time.

Now, take a good look at that list and congratulate yourself! You have probably achieved far more than you thought. It's important to recognise your own achievements because this can help you start turning 'I can't' into 'I CAN'.

As of today, start keeping a 'positive achievements' diary. Write down in it:

- everything that's made you feel good, from a good TV programme or song to something someone said or did
- anything you enjoyed doing, from eating a meal or styling your hair to playing the guitar or writing a poem
- ways you have coped with hassles or problems
- things that took courage
- new friends/relationships
- improved relationships
- ways you have helped other people

- progress with anything at home, school or work
- completed tasks or projects
- new activities.

Just the act of remembering these things and writing them down will make you feel much more positive about yourself and your life.

CELEBRATE YOUR STRENGTHS

If your self-esteem has got a bit low, it's likely that you are ignoring your good characteristics and dwelling on what you see as the bad or negative ones. This may have become a habit if most of the 'feedback' you've had in the past has been negative. It's hard to think positively about yourself if the people around you keep pointing out your shortcomings and mistakes but never celebrate your strengths. Recognising your good qualities is a very important part of building self-esteem. So identify some from this list, or write your own:

- Adaptable, Adventurous, Affectionate, Ambitious, Artistic, Attractive
- Balanced, Bright, Broad-minded
- Calm, Careful, Caring, Considerate, Courageous, Creative, Curious
- Determined, Dependable
- Easygoing, Energetic, Enthusiastic
- Faithful, Friendly, Fun, Funny
- Generous, Gentle, Good-natured
- Happy, Hard-working, Helpful, Honest
- Imaginative, Independent, Intelligent, Inventive
- Kind
- Likeable, Loving, Logical
- Modest, Moderate
- Natural, Neat

- Organised, Optimistic
- Patient, Peaceful, Perceptive, Polite, Practical
- Reasonable, Relaxed, Resourceful, Responsible, Romantic
- Sexy, Sincere, Sociable, Strong, Sympathetic
- Tactful, Talented, Thoughtful, Tolerant
- Understanding, Unique, Unusual
- Warm, Witty.

Of course there are hundreds more nice qualities:

*Aware … Active … Appreciative … Complimentary … Dynamic …
Glamorous … Light-hearted … Outgoing … Passionate …
Unselfish …*

and lots of them could apply to you. So write your own list and make it good and long! Then put the list somewhere where you'll see it every day, so it can keep reminding you of all the positive things about YOU.

Whenever you catch yourself feeling negative or insecure, read through your 'positive achievements' and 'good qualities' lists, and allow the messages they give you to firmly CANCEL OUT any negative ones.

DEALING WITH 'FAILURE'

There's literally nobody who can honestly claim never to have messed up in anything. Failures and mistakes are just a part of life. But if you take failure too seriously or see it as confirmation that you're no good/useless/hopeless/never going to succeed, you'll find it more and more difficult to try again or take on new challenges.

Someone once said: 'If you want to increase your success rate, double your failure rate'. What they meant was that in order to succeed, we have to learn from our failures – in other words, every failure is like a stepping stone on the road to success.

These days there's a lot of pressure on young people to succeed. Some of it comes from parents and teachers, and quite a lot comes from friends or your peer group. You're expected to do well in tests, get good grades, excel in sport, win talent competitions and be a wow with the opposite sex. And if you don't fulfil one or all of these expectations, it's easy to start thinking of yourself as a 'failure'.

Well, here's a comforting fact: surveys show that the happiest people are those who don't think failure matters. They just accept it, learn from it, then move cheerfully on to the next thing. They instinctively know that it's not worth beating yourself up or making a big deal about setbacks or disappointments that will soon be forgotten. Failing at something does not mean *you* are a failure.

Parents' expectations can sometimes be a problem here. Parents don't help their teenagers by pushing them too hard, so it's crucial to try and detach yourself from what other people expect. The only important thing, for your self-esteem, is to know you've had a go and done your best. If that's not enough, too bad. Forget about it, move on. Often it's not the so-called 'failure' that makes young people feel bad, but being criticised or made to feel you've let someone down. Ideally, both you and the people around you should try to make sure you come out of every experience with a positive attitude.

> **For a closer look at dealing with your parents, see**
> ***Real Life Issues: Sex and Relationships.***

It may be harder to dismiss a failure if most of your friends seem to have done better. But just remember that you are you, they are them, and there is nothing to be gained from comparing. In years to come you may be ten times more happy and contented than they are – just because you've learned to ignore failure and focus on your successes!

MIX WITH POSITIVE PEOPLE

The people you spend time with influence your thoughts, actions and behaviour. This means that anyone who puts you or your ideas down is likely to lower your self-esteem. Unfortunately, we can't always avoid negative people, especially if we work with them or they are part of

TIP BOX

Next time you are aware that you've made a mistake or not achieved what you wanted to achieve, don't waste your energy on anger or disappointment. Every mistake provides an opportunity for you to learn something useful and move on. For example, if you leave your bike un-padlocked in the street and it gets stolen, feeling furious with yourself won't achieve anything. Instead of that, think about the lesson you've learnt and make yourself a promise that if, in the future, you get another bike, you won't let it happen again. This technique is also useful if you fail an exam or don't do well in a competition. Just think 'What has that taught me?' and put the experience to good use.

our family. But it's important to be aware of their effect on you and to spend as little time as possible with them.

On the other hand, when you are surrounded by positive, supportive people, you feel better about yourself and this helps to raise your self-esteem. So try to create a personal 'support network' of positive people who make you feel good. It may help to make a list of the supportive and non-supportive people around you.

'When I was young, I found it hard with my speech. Writing and singing songs was my only means of expression, the only way to get out what was in me. Having a problem all your life and finding something that works, it's really great. It changes your whole life and makes you feel a lot better about yourself.' **Gareth Gates, singer,** on coping with being someone who stammers

CHAPTER EIGHT:

BE KIND TO YOURSELF
Turning negative thoughts into affirmations

If your self-esteem and confidence are low, you tend not to give yourself credit for all the good things you do, and to beat yourself up when anything goes wrong. This is often because you are listening to an 'inner critic' who always thinks negatively and never thinks positively.

This 'inner critic' is actually you, but the things it says have come from somewhere else. Perhaps other people have said negative things to you in the past, and you've got so used to them that you've begun 'agreeing' with them inside your own head, even though they are *not true* . Maybe you've been told over and over again that you're 'lazy' or 'careless' or 'clumsy', or that you're not as clever or nice-looking as your brother or sister. People often say these things without thinking or meaning them. They may also say them because they're in a bad mood or annoyed, or because they're jealous. Or they may have issues in their own lives that drive them to say unkind things. However, we are not concerned with their problems, but with yours. And if you've got used to being told you are 'rubbish', you may have started talking to yourself in the same way.

For example, when you make a mistake, you may say things like:

- You moron! How could you be so stupid!
- This is just typical of me.
- I've done it again – I'm a born loser!
- I never get anything right.
- Why do I bother? I know it won't work out.
- I made this happen.

Getting angry with yourself occasionally is natural. But if you call yourself names every time something goes pear-shaped, what you are actually doing is telling yourself that you don't respect yourself. And the more you do it, the more it becomes habit. So you end up just like Eeyore in *Winnie the Pooh,* always looking on the dark side and never expecting anything nice to happen.

If this sounds at all like you, it's time to start listening to what you say when you make a mistake or things go wrong. And if it's always negative or self-critical, practise turning it into something more positive. Here are some examples of positive thoughts to replace the miserable ones:

- I won't do that again!
- I'm too clever to have done that!
- At least I had a go!
- You can't win 'em all!
- I've learnt something from that.
- Better luck next time!
- That person's got a problem, so I'll ignore them.
- I know I'm not to blame.
- This is nothing to do with me – bad things can happen to good people

■ I'm glad I tried.

AFFIRMATIONS

Some people find it helps to have positive phrases to use as 'affirmations'. Affirmations are short statements you can use to replace negative thoughts with positive ones. The more you say them, the more you realise they are true. Some people pin their affirmations to the mirror, or repeat them three times every morning when they wake up.

Affirmations should directly contradict anything negative you tell yourself and they should always say what you *are,* not what you're not. For example if you catch yourself saying, 'I am an idiot', your affirmation should be 'I am intelligent' (not 'I am not an idiot').

Here are some other examples:

NEGATIVE THOUGHT	AFFIRMATION
I never do anything right	I am a capable person
No one could ever fancy me	I am attractive and special
I don't like myself	I love and appreciate myself
I don't like my nose/ears/legs/face/weight	I like and accept my own body
Nothing good ever happens to me	I deserve good things
I can't make friends	I am a friendly and lovable person

All these affirmations are the kind of things that people with good self-esteem automatically feel about themselves. They are not conceited or unrealistic. An unrealistic affirmation might be: 'I am the cleverest and most beautiful person in the world' – though feel free to try that one and see if it works!

Don't be impatient with your affirmations because the more you use them the more they will become part of you. Always use one immediately after any negative thought. For example next time you lose or drop something and catch yourself saying, 'I'm really clumsy!' or, 'That's just like me!' stop right there and cancel that thought with: **'I have a perfect right to lose/drop things, it's normal.'**

WHAT DO YOU ENJOY?

None of us is much good at things we don't enjoy or that we find very difficult. For instance, if you hate Maths or French or Science, you probably won't be brilliant at them. We can't all enjoy or be good at everything. So there's no need to feel bad about being hopeless at things that just don't grab you.

But it is important to recognise the activities that make you feel *good*. Usually these are things you like doing or things you do well – although of course you don't have to be good at everything you enjoy.

Make a list of all the things you enjoy or are good at. This can include anything from having a laugh with friends or computer games to mending bicycles or playing the violin (but not anything that's dangerous or damaging to you or to other people).

This is your 'positive activities' list, and it's there to remind you that you are, in fact an active, positive person who is good at things. It doesn't matter what other people think of these activities – the point is that you enjoy them. Some of the world's greatest inventors spent time doing things that other people thought were a waste of time! It's important to spend lots of time doing the things you enjoy, especially when your self-esteem needs a boost.

But a word of warning: it's not good to become so obsessed with just *one* interest that it becomes almost the only thing that matters to you. Usually when people do this, it's because they don't want to get to grips with real life or their own feelings.

DON'T DEMAND TOO MUCH OF YOURSELF

It's difficult to have confidence or self-esteem if you constantly demand perfection of yourself and then fail to measure up to your own standards! Perfection is a high goal to aim for, so don't insist on starting there, or even arriving there. The important thing is to do your best and to have some fun along the way.

Let's take four extreme examples. You want to be a top footballer, a model, a pop singer or a chef. To you, this means equalling David Beckham, Naomi Campbell, Will Young or Jamie Oliver. You join a team, start singing, get some fashion pictures taken or enter a cooking contest. Then after a while you become discouraged or disappointed because you haven't been 'discovered'. You then either label yourself a failure or start blaming other people for not recognising your talent. Either way, you don't feel good about yourself!

This would all be different if you had set yourself *realistic* goals to begin with. These might be:

- to play as much football as you can
- to develop your interest in fashion and beauty
- to take music lessons and perform in public as much as you can

■ to become a more skilled/adventurous cook.

These are all achievable goals. When you reach them, pat yourself on the back and set yourself another achievable goal – entering a local trial or competition for example. The goal is to become confident enough to *enter* a competition. You don't have to win it. If you do, though, then you can set yourself another realistic goal.

There's nothing wrong with ambition or believing the sky's the limit. But there's a lot wrong with expecting instant perfection and then hating yourself for failing to achieve it. Setting yourself one realistic goal at a time gives you the chance of lots of small successes, which will in turn build up your confidence.

If a day comes when it looks like you're not going to get much further, congratulate yourself for all your achievements so far and, above all, go on enjoying and developing your talent and finding ways to enjoy it.

TIP BOX

As well as being kind to yourself, try being kind to someone else. It's amazing the effect that giving someone a helping hand or listening to their problems can have on your self-esteem. This doesn't mean you should do for others what they should be doing for themselves (like their homework!), but making a positive contribution to someone else will give you a sense of achievement and a lovely warm glow.

CHAPTER NINE:

QUIZ: HOW CONFIDENT DO YOU FEEL?
How much faith do you have in yourself?

Confidence and self-esteem are closely related, but they do not always go hand in hand. Feeling OK about yourself *inside* does not automatically translate into confidence in your dealings with other people – and being able to put on a confident 'front' does not always mean you have good self-esteem. But the ability to behave confidently is very useful in life.

Your answers to this simple Confidence Quiz will reveal just how much faith you have in yourself. There's no 'right' score because we all lack confidence in some situations, but your answers will reveal where you most need to build up your confidence techniques.

HOW CONFIDENT DO YOU FEEL?

1 *When you meet new people, can you talk to them quite easily?*

2 *How do you feel if you have to stand up and say something?*

3 *Do you enjoy performing in a play or concert?*

4 *Are you able to be natural in an interview?*

5 *If you're sure about something, can you argue your case?*

6 *Do you hate reading aloud to a group, even though you have no problem reading?*

7 *Can you keep smiling when you're a bit unsure inside?*

8 *In an embarrassing situation do you think 'I can cope' or 'Help!'?*

9 *Are you afraid of letting yourself down in public?*

10 *Do you feel awkward and tongue-tied when you fancy someone?*

11 *Can you stand up for what you believe in when others disagree?*

12 *Can you mix easily at parties?*

Don't worry if some or all your answers reveal a lack of self-confidence because Chapter 10 is all about how to feel more sure of yourself in 'public' situations.

CHAPTER TEN:

CREATING CONFIDENCE
Feeling comfortable with yourself

Confidence has nothing to do with being good-looking, clever, loud, rich, sporty, popular or talented. It's just to do with feeling comfortable with yourself and not being worried about what other people think.

There are two sorts of confidence: **inner confidence** (which is all about self-esteem) and **outer confidence**, which helps you feel comfortable with other people. Although the two are closely linked, this chapter is mainly about outer confidence – the kind that helps in your dealings with others.

Outer confidence is all about believing in yourself – or at least *acting* as if you believe in yourself, so you don't appear awkward or nervous. It's easier to have outer confidence when you are sure of your ability or when you feel you have other people's approval. It's more difficult when you are with people who are not supportive or when you doubt your own ability.

Luckily, there are techniques that can help raise your outer confidence, even when you are feeling a bit unsure inside. And one of the simplest of these is to *look happy*. OK, that's not always easy, but it's amazing how just putting a smile on your face and looking relaxed and alert can convince other people that you are in control. It can also be a good way to disarm bullies because the last thing bullies expect is for their victims to be friendly (but don't let a bully mistake this friendliness for a willingness to go along with anything he or she says).

> **For a closer look at bullying, see**
> ***Real Life Issues: Bullying.***

No one feels confident all the time. But it's good to appear confident in everyday situations, so you can:

- express your own opinion
- say 'no' and stick to it
- stand up for yourself
- feel comfortable meeting new people
- make new friends
- join in new activities.

And the great thing about learning to look confident is that it helps you *feel* confident as well.

Often, when young people feel nervous or unsure, well-meaning friends and relatives tell them, 'Just be yourself' – as if this was really easy. The truth is, it's very hard to act naturally when you feel self-conscious. You may be so overtaken by anxiety, or even panic, that you can't concentrate properly on what other people are saying and doing. So your responses feel geeky or unnatural.

Although this is annoying, there's nothing unusual about it and it may even indicate that you are more sensitive and aware than the kind of people who never suffer a moment's self-doubt. But if your feelings of self-consciousness are so strong that they stop you doing things, you should practise some techniques that will help you take your attention off yourself and focus it on other people or on what you are doing.

An important first step is to improve your posture – the way you sit, stand and move – as this will help you look the part:

- Stand tall. Imagine there's a strong invisible thread pulling you up from the top of your head so your whole body is lifted and in line.
- Lengthen your neck, keeping your chin tucked in.
- Avoid nervous, fidgety movements. If necessary, keep your hands loosely clasped.
- Walk with a spring in your step.
- Make eye contact with people.
- Smile – unless there is a good reason not to!
- Breathe slowly and deeply.

The following techniques can also help when you feel self-conscious in a social situation:

- Find a nearby object to examine, as this will immediately take your mind off yourself. For example, study the pattern on the wallpaper or a detail in a picture. Do really *look* at it and perhaps count things in it. But keep your head level – don't choose something down on the floor or high above your head.
- Find yourself a specific task to do, like tidying or rearranging something.
- Think about something that always makes you feel good – like your best friend, your dog or your favourite place.
- Some people find it helps to sing a song or say a rhyme inside your

head. The object is to occupy your thoughts until the feelings of anxiety pass and you can get fully involved in whatever is going on.

■ If you're supposed to be chatting, make an effort to concentrate on the other person rather than on yourself. Ask them questions and listen very carefully to their answers, as if you had to memorise them. *Remember – if you're standing tall, looking calm and smiling, no one can tell that you don't feel confident.*

■ Learn from someone who always seems confident. How do they act? What is it they do that makes them seem confident?

BODY IMAGE

People talk about their bodies an awful lot, and they never seem to be happy with the one they've got. Some even think that 'if only' they could change the way they look, they would be happy and confident. But, of course, *this is not true*. The secret of feeling good about yourself is to like and accept yourself – just as you are.

Your body-image (the way you see yourself) is very closely bound up with your self-esteem. It includes:

■ what you think you look like
■ how you think others see you
■ how much you like and accept your appearance.

If you have a poor body-image it can affect your confidence and your relationships. But you can improve your body-image in lots of ways:

■ List all the things you like about your appearance.
■ List all the compliments you've received.
■ Dress to emphasise the parts of your body you like best.
■ Make any simple changes that you think would help you – for example to your clothes, hair and general appearance.

■ Accept the things about you that are less than perfect and stop worrying about them.

■ Break free of your body-image if you feel it is limiting you. Acting differently will change how you see yourself and how others see you.

■ Try to take your appearance less seriously!

It's completely pointless to compare yourself with film and TV stars who have spent a fortune on their hair, teeth, clothes and make-up or endured painful surgery to change the bits of themselves they don't

TIP BOX

Confidence is especially important at interviews. So much so that short-sighted employers often end up giving jobs to people who 'perform' well, rather than to people who would be good at the job. If you find interviews an ordeal, here are some tips to help give you an air of confidence:

■ *do lots of advance preparation, so you are ready with all the answers*

■ *make friendly eye contact with the person you are speaking to*

■ *keep fidgeting and gesticulations to a minimum*

■ *remember to blow your own trumpet – they won't know what's special about you if you don't tell them!*

■ *sound positive and never ever draw attention to aspects of yourself you don't like.*

like. The reason it's pointless is because, first, these people don't look *nearly* so fantastic in real life and, second, no amount of nips, tucks and designer clothes can make you feel good inside – as so many of the rich and famous keep proving.

Bear in mind, too, that lots of women don't like musclemen and lots of men couldn't care less about the size of a girl's boobs. What really matters is the person inside.

Your body deserves to be loved and cared for, and this means a healthy diet and a healthy lifestyle (see Chapter 12). Not liking your body is like not liking yourself. And trying to change it by over-exercising or under-eating is not only dangerous for your health but very bad for your self-esteem.

> **For a closer look at creating a positive body image, see *Real Life Issues: Eating Disorders.***

Remember, too, that in adolescence your body is constantly changing. Your clothes may suddenly become too short, too tight or too loose; your skin may break out in spots; your hair may develop a mind of its own. Sometimes you won't be delighted with the way you look. But keep reminding yourself that you have something special and unique to offer, and it's not always visible on the outside.

CHAPTER ELEVEN:

MAKING FRIENDS
... *by 'acting friendly'*

Friends are good to have around. They laugh at your jokes and cheer you up when you're feeling low. You don't need loads of them, but we all need one or two good friends who we feel easy with. Not having any friends can make you feel very lonely, especially when it seems like everyone else has got someone to go places and do things with.

Making friends may seem a simple thing, but it doesn't just happen automatically. In order to make friends, you have to 'act friendly', and this is always more difficult if you feel shy or unsure of yourself.

Acting friendly means:

- smiling, even when you're not feeling great
- saying 'hi' first, and not always waiting for the other person to talk to you
- being a good listener
- asking questions, and listening to the answers
- not moaning – talking about good things as well as bad
- sharing and being generous.

Sometimes, if you've been bullied or left out in the past, or if friendships have gone wrong, it can seem as if nobody wants to be your friend. This is never really true, but sometimes it takes a new beginning, like a change of school or a change of scene, to make new friendships happen. New people take you just as they find you. Past experiences don't matter because in a new place you are a new you – friendly, confident and full of self-esteem!

WHAT MAKES A FRIEND?

Friendship is about enjoying someone's company – you like being with them and they like being with you. Here are some of the qualities that people look for in a friend:

- a sense of humour
- the ability to laugh and have fun
- loyalty
- fairness
- a sympathetic nature
- kindness
- good at thinking of things to do
- good at taking turns and sharing
- good at giving compliments (that they really mean!).

To make new friends (including boyfriends and girlfriends), you need to work on your **'people skills'** because these can help you to reach out and make contact with others. People skills are very similar to assertiveness skills (see Chapter 5). For example:

- Make friendly eye contact with people.
- Pay attention to what they say.
- Remember: 'I matter and so do you.'

- Make sure your posture and your facial expression tell the world that you respect yourself.
- Practise some opening lines. Questions are always good, but make them neutral ('Did you see …?' or 'What do you think of …?'), not nosy or personal.

Your mates don't have to be just like you; in fact, it's much more interesting if they have their own thoughts and opinions. But you do need something in common – an interest, an outlook, a sense of humour, a football team … Even so, some friendships just don't work out, and sometimes people who used to be friends discover they no longer have anything in common. A friendship can last a day, a month, a year or a lifetime.

Remember that if someone doesn't want to be friends with you, it's not because there is anything wrong with you. We can't all be friends with everyone, and there may be lots of personal reasons why someone feels they can't handle a new friend (even someone as cool as you!) right now.

ALONE NEED NOT BE LONELY

Although most young people like to have friends, many others prefer their own company. People like this are happy doing things on their own and don't feel the need to be surrounded by friends. They may have plenty of confidence and self-esteem, but be choosy about who they spend time with and not interested in proving they are 'popular'. Perhaps they find teen talk boring and have other things they want to do. There is certainly nothing 'weird' about preferring your own company in your teens, though as time goes on you will probably find more opportunities to mix with the kind of people you like.

WATCH OUT FOR FALSE FRIENDS

However much you want to be accepted as part of a group, remember that real friends don't get you into trouble or ask you to do things you don't want to do, like joy-ride, bully someone or take drugs. Occasionally, a so-called friend may say that if you don't join in some dangerous activity, like stealing or shoplifting, they won't be your friend any more. Well, that's the kind of friend you'd be a whole lot better off without!

How not to make friends

There are some kinds of behaviour that you may possibly get away with at home (though you shouldn't!) but which will definitely put off potential friends. These include:

- lying or cheating
- criticising people behind their backs
- boasting, or claiming credit for something you didn't do
- being bossy
- criticising the way people do things
- being too intense or serious
- talking about yourself too much
- moaning and being sorry for yourself
- being mean.

DAVE'S STORY

'When I was 14, our family moved to south London from Belfast, and I had to start at a new school. I'd had quite a few friends at my old school, but I couldn't seem to make any at the new one because most of the kids in my year had already got their friends and they hung about in their own groups. I know I should have tried to get to

know people and join in, but I couldn't really be bothered. I felt too self-conscious, and I got teased about my Belfast accent. In the end, I decided I didn't care and I just kept myself to myself.

'Mum kept saying I should invite someone from school to our house, but there was no one I wanted to ask. I know my parents were worried because they went in to talk to my class teacher about it, and afterwards he tried to get me to mix in more, but it didn't work. I felt I didn't have much to say to people. I'm not interested in Arsenal or EastEnders, which was all most of them talked about, so I felt like some kind of alien. Luckily, I get on with my mum and dad and sister, so life at home was OK, but I had to keep reminding myself that I had really good mates back in Belfast. I didn't admit it to anyone, but I felt lonely.

TIP BOX

One of the best things about a good friend is that they're interested in the things you say. This works both ways, so if you want to make new friends you need to get good at listening to people and responding to their thoughts and ideas. Cracking jokes and making people laugh is an easy way to get accepted, but it's really only half of what friendship is about. The other half is about sharing problems and supporting each other through thick and thin. One reason some people turn into bullies is because they're only interested in themselves and have difficulty making real friends.

'After GCSEs, I went to do a BTEC in Music Technology at college, and I made up my mind before term started that I was going to be really friendly to the other students because it was a new beginning and I didn't want to go on being how I was at school. I wanted to be like how I'd been at my old school in Belfast, more jokey and not bothered about things. At first, it felt quite like 'acting' because I'd got used to not smiling or saying much. But it wasn't as hard as I thought because we were all new and people wanted to make friends.

'Probably what made the most difference was that I had a different attitude. I made myself chat to people and ask questions and be more friendly. Anyway, it worked because I got included in things from the start and felt I was part of the group. It was a really good feeling. I'm much more easy with people now, so it's not like I'm acting anymore. And I've got some good mates to go out with, so my mum has stopped thinking I'm a freak!' **Dave, 19**

For a closer look at friendships, see
Real Life Issues: Sex and Relationships.

CHAPTER TWELVE:

HEALTH MATTERS
Caring for your body

Despite the stereotype image, plenty of teenagers *don't* spend their lives slouched in an armchair watching TV, playing video games, eating junk food and never taking any exercise. In fact, more and more young people are becoming aware of health and environmental issues and understand that their bodies are affected by the way they live.

Not caring for your body is like not caring for yourself, so it's an important part of self-esteem. When you're young it's easy to think that your body is strong enough to take anything – too much or too little food, no exercise, junk food, drugs, alcohol or not enough sleep. But the truth is that everything you do to your body, good and bad, has a knock-on effect – either now or later in life, or both. And it's hard to feel good about yourself or your life if you don't treat your body the way it deserves.

YOU ARE WHAT YOU EAT

Teenagers need more calories than adults to supply the energy their bodies need to finish growing. That means lots of food, but it has to be the right kind of food. Fast food like burgers, crisps, chips, chocolate bars and pot noodles is OK from time to time as a lazy treat, but it's not good every day because it doesn't contain all the nourishing things your body needs, and usually includes unhealthy amounts of fat, salt and sugar.

To have enough energy for life and to keep your body healthy, your everyday diet should include:

plenty of –

■ bread, cereals, pasta, rice and potatoes
■ fruit and vegetables, including root vegetables and green vegetables.

medium amounts of –

■ protein foods, such as chicken, meat, fish, eggs, milk, yoghurt, cheese, nuts and beans.

only small amounts of –

■ fatty foods, such as butter, margarine, cream and oil
■ fried food, such as chips and fry-ups
■ sugary things, such as fizzy drinks, sweets, cakes, biscuits and ice cream.

Health experts say that at least half your calories should come from things in the 'plenty of' group and at least a third from the 'medium amounts' group. So that means less than a quarter of your calories should come from the 'small amounts' group. Remember that many things in this group (like a chocolate bar or a packet of crisps) look small in size but can actually contain more fat, sugar and calories than a whole plate of, say, roast chicken, jacket potato and peas.

EATING TOO LITTLE

Most young people enjoy their food and don't eat a great deal more or less than their body needs. But a very few people use food as a way of dealing with personal problems. For example, people with anorexia (the medical word for deliberately starving yourself) develop a fear of being fat that goes way, way beyond normal dieting. The need to control their weight dominates all other feelings, so in a way they are using it to try to escape other problems. In reality, of course, it doesn't help with other problems, but it does cause serious health problems, including infertility, kidney damage, poor circulation, brittle bones, fainting and dizziness. It can even be fatal.

Another harmful condition, bulimia, also results from an obsessive desire to be skinny. But instead of not eating, the person binges on food and then gets rid of it by being sick. It's important for anyone who thinks they may have either anorexia or bulimia to talk about it with someone they trust and seek help from a counsellor or doctor.

> **For a closer look at anorexia and bulimia, see**
> ***Real Life Issues: Eating Disorders.***

EATING TOO MUCH

If weight gain becomes a problem in your teens, the best way to control it is to stick to the everyday healthy-eating guidelines above. This is much easier if everyone else in your family is eating healthily too, so ask whoever does the shopping not to keep the cupboards full of tempting foods that are high in fat or sugar. Small changes to your diet, such as cutting out snacks and high-fat foods, can make a real difference. It's much better to control your weight through healthy eating and regular exercise than through diets. Most weight lost through 'slimming' diets is put straight back on when you give them up.

EATING AND SELF-ESTEEM

Most teenage eating disorders – from anorexia to 'comfort eating' – are directly connected with self-esteem. What happens is that the person starts to feel bad about himself or herself (for any of the reasons given in Chapter 3) and then mistakenly chooses food as a way to deal with this.

Compulsive eating may start as a way to comfort feelings of distress, but of course this can lead to obesity if you are eating far more than you need.

Anorexia may develop if a young person blames their feelings of low self-esteem on the fact that they are not as thin as the skinniest supermodel. Magazines are partly to blame for this as they encourage us to feel that we're not attractive unless we are unhealthily skinny. This is rubbish, of course, but if someone who already feels they're not worth much starts believing it, then it's only a short step to thinking everything would be all right if they stopped eating.

The result is they end up unattractively and dangerously thin, but with

FACT BOX

■ *Never dash out of the house with an empty stomach. Try to eat a good breakfast, such as wholegrain cereal and fresh fruit, every day.*

■ *Prepare a healthy, delicious packed lunch to help you avoid the temptation of junk snacks. Include things you really love – for example, pasta salad, a chicken or egg and cress wholemeal sandwich and your favourite fruit yoghurt.*

no more self-esteem than before because the real problem was to do with not loving and respecting themselves. That's why it's so important to develop a positive self-image and to keep your body looking its best through healthy eating and regular exercise.

DRUGS AND ALCOHOL

Any kind of addiction is damaging to your self-esteem because you are not in control of your own behaviour. Your brain knows what you are doing is bad, but your body feels it can't do without it, so you lose all respect for yourself.

People often begin to use drugs or drink a lot of alcohol to escape things that make them feel bad, like stress in the family, relationship hassles or feeling different from everyone else. The problem is that when the effect of the drugs or alcohol wears off, you feel even worse than you did before, so you are tempted to take more. And this leads to addiction. Once you are addicted, drugs and alcohol start being the only thing you think about, so you may stop caring about friends and family and even commit crimes to get money for your habit. You may also cause serious harm to other people through negligence or accidents.

So if you think you or a friend are addicted, it's very important to admit there is a problem and find the right kind of help. Any of the organisations listed on pages 76–77 will understand your concern and be able to advise you.

Cigarettes are also a form of addiction, even though (like alcohol) they are not illegal. Smoking reduces your level of fitness, has very bad long-term effects on your skin, heart, lungs and circulation, and is horrendously expensive.

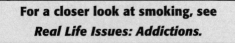

For a closer look at smoking, see
Real Life Issues: Addictions.

ENJOY EXERCISE

Exercise increases your sense of well-being in lots of different ways:

- It helps you 'let off steam', so it's a good outlet for anger or frustration.
- It stimulates the 'feel-good' chemicals in your body.
- It relieves anxiety and helps you relax.
- It helps you sleep better.
- It strengthens your whole body and helps to prevent illnesses.

Always choose a sport or exercise you enjoy as this will give you a positive sense of achievement, and try to exercise regularly rather than in occasional spurts.

TRY RELAXATION

Some people can switch off their anxieties very easily just by calling a friend, watching TV or listening to a CD. If you can't, try this relaxation exercise:

- Choose a quiet place where you won't be interrupted.
- Make yourself very comfortable by either sitting or lying down.
- Start to breathe slowly and deeply, in a calm, easy way.
- Gently tense, then relax, each part of your body, starting with your feet and working your way up to your face and head.
- As you focus on each area, think of warmth, heaviness and relaxation.
- Push any distracting thoughts to the back of your mind – imagine them floating away and let your mind go empty.
- Stay like this for about 20 minutes, then take some deep breaths and open your eyes, but stay sitting or lying for a short time before you get up.

> **For a closer look at managing stress, see**
> ***Real Life Issues: Stress.***

EXPRESS YOURSELF

Any kind of creativity, like dance, drama, music or writing, will build your confidence by encouraging you to express your emotions, understand your own feelings and explore ways of dealing with people or relationships. Most schools and colleges offer opportunities to try these things. If yours doesn't, ask your local library if they have information about any clubs or classes you could join. If you have left school, you could try an evening class at your local adult college.

'I like to do active things and I take my health and fitness quite seriously. There are no downsides to being fit – everyone's a winner. And if you can find a team sport to join in with, it can work wonders for your confidence and social skills, too.'

Josie D'Arby, TV presenter and actress

Final Word

I hope this book has shown you that you have more power over your life than you thought. Developing confidence and self-esteem is a gradual thing and it probably won't happen overnight. But you *can* take charge of your own life and you *can* deal with the rest of the world on equal terms. The power will come through recognising your own unique worth and remembering the importance of: 'I matter, and so do you.'

HELPFUL ORGANISATIONS

Sometimes you can feel so low or your situation can seem so hopeless that you don't know where to turn or whom to speak to. Here are some organisations that can help. Don't suffer in silence, give them a call – they may just be able to make a difference.

CARELINE

Tel: 020 8514 1177 (Mon–Fri 10am–4pm and 7pm–10pm)

Confidential crisis counselling for children, young people and adults. Careline can refer you to other organisations and support groups throughout the country.

CHILDLINE

Freepost 1111
London N1 0BR
Helpline: 0800 1111
www.childline.org.uk

The UK's 24-hour helpline for children and young people with any problem.

EATING DISORDERS ASSOCIATION
First Floor, Wensum House
103 Prince of Wales Road
Norwich NR1 1DW
Helpline: 01603 664914
www.edauk.com

Helplines, information and a nationwide network of self-help groups.

GET CONNECTED
Tel: 0808 808 4994 (1pm–11pm every day)
Email: help@getconnected.org.uk

Free UK-wide helpline and email service that finds young people the best help, whatever the problem.

SAMARITANS
Tel: 08457 90 90 90

If you need to talk to someone urgently, the Samaritans offer support 24 hours a day.

YOUNG MINDS
102–108 Clerkenwell Road
London EC1M 5SA
Tel: 020 7336 8445
www.youngminds.org.uk

National charity that works to promote the mental well-being of children and young people.